MORE SONGS OF THE TWENTIES

THE DECADE SERIES

ISBN 0-7935-3091-1

HAL•LEONARD™
CORPORATION
7777 W. BLUEMOUND RD. P.O. BOX 13819 MILWAUKEE, WI 53213

Contents

4	After You Get What You Want You Don't Want It
10	Ain't We Got Fun?
13	Alabamy Bound
16	All By Myself
20	Amapola (Pretty Little Poppy)
22	Angela Mia
26	Any Time
34	Baby, Won't You Please Come Home
28	Bill
30	Bye Bye Blackbird
37	Can't Help Lovin' Dat Man
40	Carolina In The Morning
48	Cecilia (Does Your Mother Know You're Out)
50	Charleston
43	Crazy Blues
54	Don't Ever Leave Me
57	Everybody Step
62	Fascinating Rhythm
66	Good News
70	The Hawaiian Wedding Song (Ke Kali Nei Au)
73	How About Me?
76	I Want To Be Bad
80	I Want To Be Happy
84	I'll Get By (As Long As I Have You)
86	I'm Just Wild About Harry
88	If I Had A Talking Picture Of You
96	Lazy
91	Let Me Sing And I'm Happy
100	Limehouse Blues
102	Louise
104	Love Me Or Leave Me
108	Malagueña
114	The Man I Love
118	Mexicali Rose
121	Mountain Greenery
128	My Blue Heaven
136	My Heart Stood Still
140	My Yiddishe Momme
144	Neapolitan Nights
148	Nobody Knows You When You're Down And Out
150	Say It With Music
154	Someone To Watch Over Me
158	The Song Is Ended (But The Melody Lingers On)
162	Sunny
166	Sunny Side Up
6	Tain't Nobody's Biz-ness If I Do
168	Thou Swell
172	What'll I Do?
131	Whip-Poor-Will
190	Who?
176	With A Song In My Heart
180	Yes Sir, That's My Baby
184	You Are Love

AFTER YOU GET WHAT YOU WANT YOU DON'T WANT IT

Words and Music by
IRVING BERLIN

Medium slow bounce tempo

Voice

AF - TER YOU GET WHAT YOU WANT_ YOU DON'T WANT IT,_

If I gave you the moon,_ You'd grow tired of it soon.

You're like a ba - by, you want what you want when you want it,

TAIN'T NOBODY'S BIZ-NESS IF I DO

Words and Music by PORTER GRAINGER
and EVERETT ROBBINS

AIN'T WE GOT FUN?
(From "BY THE LIGHT OF THE SILVERY MOON")

Words by GUS KAHN and RAYMOND B. EGAN
Music by RICHARD A. WHITING

ALABAMY BOUND
(From "THE GREAT AMERICAN BROADCAST")

Words by B.G. DeSYLVA and BUD GREEN
Music by RAY HENDERSON

ALL BY MYSELF

Words and Music by
IRVING BERLIN

I sit a - lone___ with a ta - ble and a chair,___ so un - hap - py there,___ play - ing sol - i - taire___ all by my - self.___ I get lone - ly,_____ watch - ing the clock___

AMAPOLA
(PRETTY LITTLE POPPY)

By JOSEPH M. LACALLE
New English Words by ALBERT GAMSE

ANGELA MIA

Words and Music by ERNO RAPEE
and LEW POLLACK

ANY TIME

Words and Music by
HERBERT HAPPY LAWSON

BILL
(From "SHOW BOAT")

Lyrics by P.G. WODEHOUSE and OSCAR HAMMERSTEIN II
Music by JEROME KERN

Moderately

BYE BYE BLACKBIRD
(From "PETE KELLY'S BLUES")

Words by MORT DIXON
Music by RAY HENDERSON

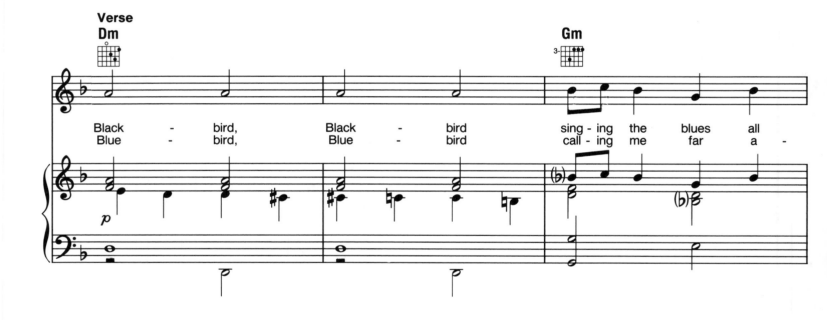

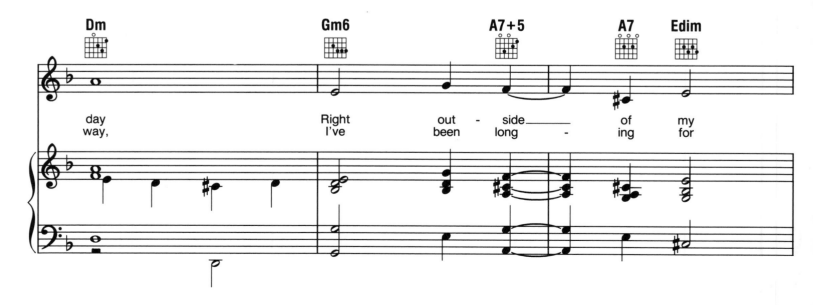

BABY, WON'T YOU PLEASE COME HOME

Words and Music by CHARLES WARFIELD
and CLARENCE WILLIAMS

CAN'T HELP LOVIN' DAT MAN

(From "SHOW BOAT")

Words by OSCAR HAMMERSTEIN II
Music by JEROME KERN

CAROLINA IN THE MORNING

Words by GUS KAHN
Music by WALTER DONALDSON

CRAZY BLUES

Words and Music by
PERRY BRADFORD

MCA music publishing

CECILIA
(DOES YOUR MOTHER KNOW YOU'RE OUT)

Words by HERMAN RUBY
Music by DAVE DREYER

CHARLESTON

Words and Music by CECIL MACK
and JIMMY JOHNSON

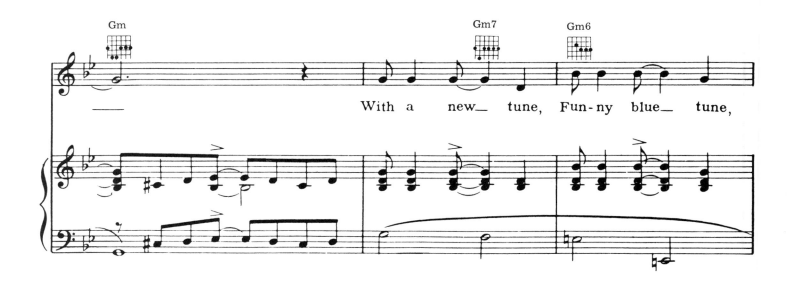

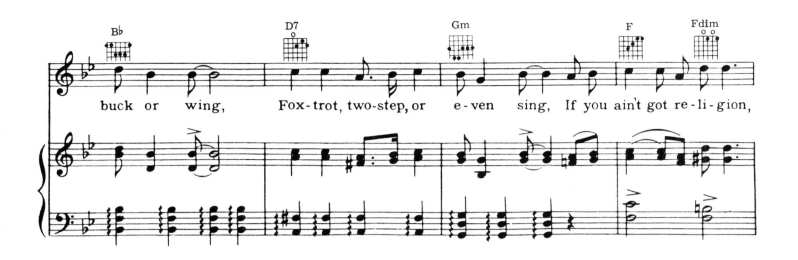

buck or wing, Fox-trot, two-step, or e-ven sing, If you ain't got re-li-gion,

in your feet, You can do this prance and do it neat.

Charles-ton! Charles-ton! Made in Car-o-lin-a,__

DON'T EVER LEAVE ME

(From "SWEET ADELINE")

Lyrics by OSCAR HAMMERSTEIN II
Music by JEROME KERN

EVERYBODY STEP

Words and Music by
IRVING BERLIN

FASCINATING RHYTHM
(From "RHAPSODY IN BLUE")

Music and Lyrics by
GEORGE and IRA GERSHWIN

out an-y warn-ing, And hangs a-round all day. I'll have to sneak up to it,

Some-day, and speak up to it, I hope it list-ens when I say:

REFRAIN

"Fas-ci-nat-ing Rhy-thm You've got me on the go! Fas-ci-nat-ing Rhy-thm I'm all a-

qui - ver. What a mess you're mak-ing! The neigh-bors want to know why I'm

GOOD NEWS

Words and Music by B.G. DeSYLVA,
LEW BROWN and RAY HENDERSON

68

THE HAWAIIAN WEDDING SONG
(KE KALI NEI AU)

English Words by AL HOFFMAN and DICK MANNING
Hawaiian Words and Music by CHARLES E. KING

Slowly, with much warmth

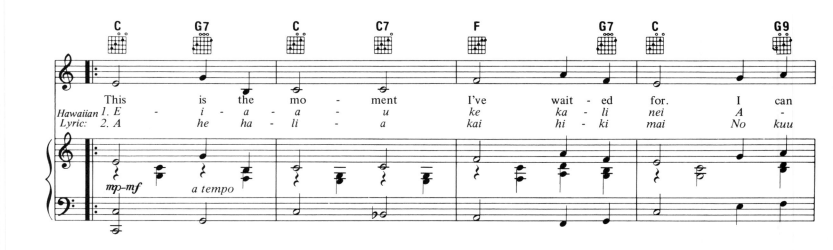

This is the mo - ment I've wait - ed for. I can

Hawaiian Lyric:
1. E - i - a - a - u ke ka - li nei A -
2. A he ha - li - a kai hi - ki mai No kuu

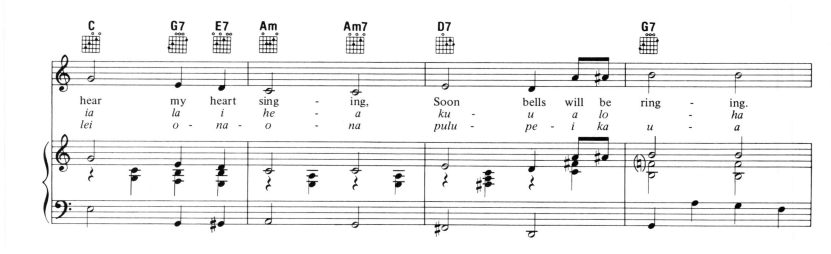

hear my heart sing - ing, Soon bells will be ring - ing.

ia la i he - a ku - u a lo - ha
lei o - na - o - na pulu - pe - i ka u - a

HOW ABOUT ME?

Words and Music by
IRVING BERLIN

I WANT TO BE BAD

(From "GOOD NEWS")

Words and Music by B.G. DeSYLVA,
LEW BROWN and RAY HENDERSON

I WANT TO BE HAPPY

Words by IRVING CAESAR
Music by VINCENT YOUMANS

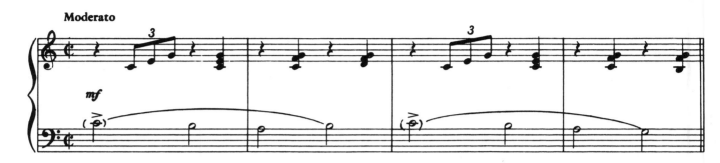

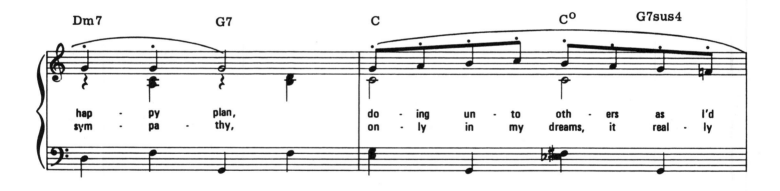

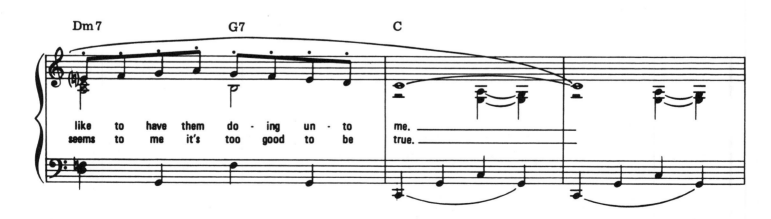

James: I'm a ver-y or-di-nar-y man, try-ing to work out life's
Nanette: No one ev-er talked like that to me, I have nev-er known such

hap-py plan, do-ing un-to oth-ers as I'd
sym-pa-thy, on-ly in my dreams, it real-ly

like to have them do-ing un-to me.
seems to me it's too good to be true.

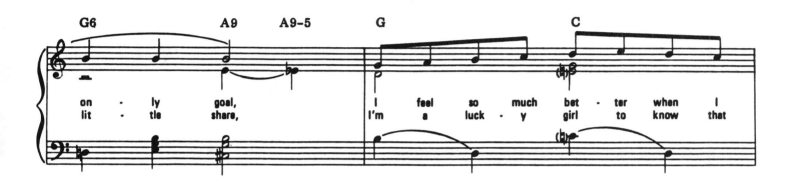

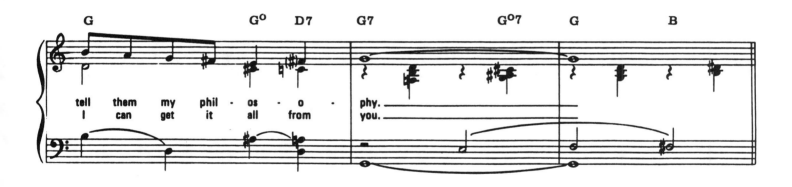

be hap - py   till I   make   you   hap - py,   too. _____

_____   Life's real - ly   worth   liv - ing,   when   we   are

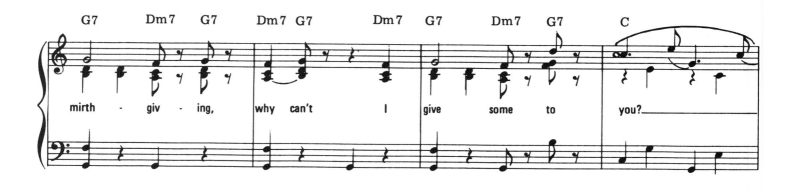

mirth - giv - ing,   why can't   I   give   some   to   you? _____

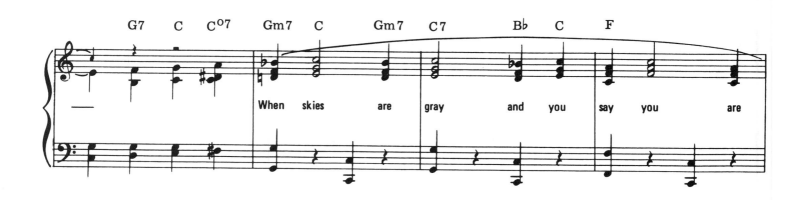

_____   When   skies   are   gray   and   you   say   you   are

I'LL GET BY
(AS LONG AS I HAVE YOU)

Words by ROY TURK
Music by FRED E. AHLERT

I'll Get By as long as I have you. Tho' there be rain and dark-ness too, I'll not com-plain, I'll

I'M JUST WILD ABOUT HARRY

Words and Music by NOBLE SISSLE
and EUBIE BLAKE

88

IF I HAD A TALKING PICTURE OF YOU

Words and Music by RAY HENDERSON,
LEW BROWN and B.G. DeSYLVA

LET ME SING AND I'M HAPPY

(From The Motion Picture "MAMMY")

Words and Music by
IRVING BERLIN

LAZY

Words and Music by
IRVING BERLIN

Ev-'ry-time _____ I see a pup-py up-
Life is short _____ and get-ting short-er with

on a sum-mer's day,
each day that goes by,

a pup-py dog at play.
and how the time does fly.

LIMEHOUSE BLUES

(From "ZIEGFELD FOLLIES")

Words by DOUGLAS FURBER
Music by PHILIP BRAHAM

LOUISE

(From The Paramount Picture "INNOCENTS OF PARIS")

Words by LEO ROBIN
Music by RICHARD A. WHITING

LOVE ME OR LEAVE ME

(From "LOVE ME OR LEAVE ME")

Lyrics by GUS KAHN
Music by WALTER DONALDSON

MALAGUEÑA

Music and Spanish Lyric by ERNESTO LECUONA
English Lyric by MARIAN BANKS

THE MAN I LOVE

Music and Lyrics by
GEORGE and IRA GERSHWIN

MEXICALI ROSE

Words by HELEN STONE
Music by JACK B. TENNEY

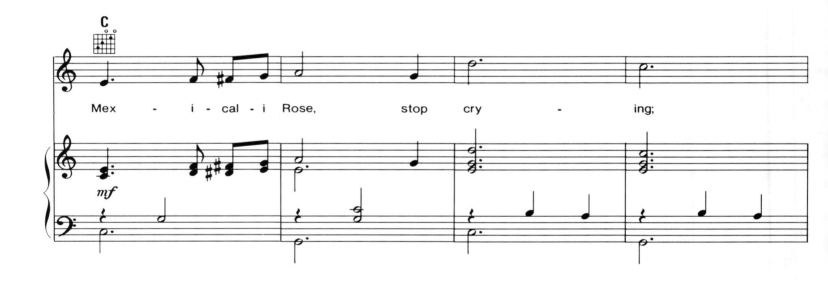

Mex - i - cal - i Rose, stop cry - ing;

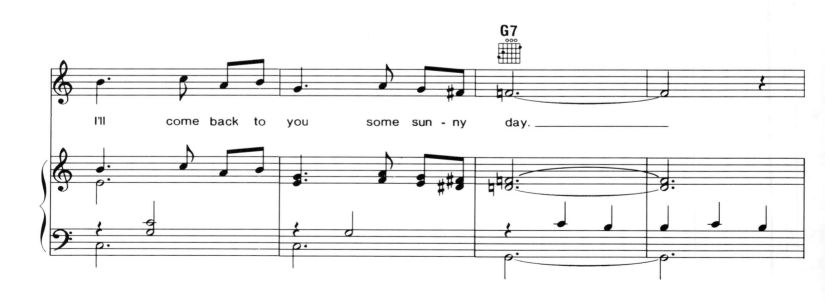

I'll come back to you some sun - ny day. _____

MCA music publishing

MOUNTAIN GREENERY
(From "THE GARRICK GAIETIES")

Words by LORENZ HART
Music by RICHARD RODGERS

126

MY BLUE HEAVEN

Words by GEORGE WHITING
Music by WALTER DONALDSON

129

WHIP-POOR-WILL
(From "SALLY")

Words by BUD DeSYLVA
Music by JEROME KERN

Mem - 'ry takes me back a - way ... To an ear - ly child - hood
While the dusk - y night bird flew ... To the eve - ning ren - dez -

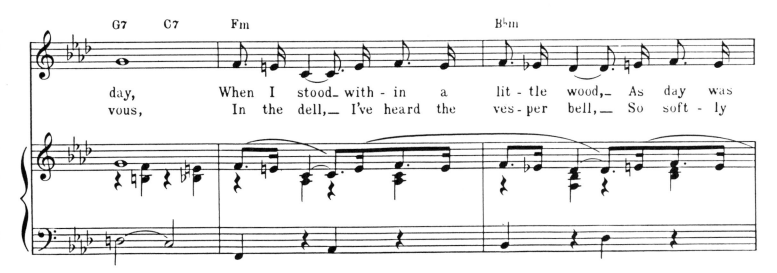

day, ... When I stood with - in a lit - tle wood, ... As day was
vous, ... In the dell, ... I've heard the ves - per bell, ... So soft - ly

132

MY HEART STOOD STILL
(From "A CONNECTICUT YANKEE")

Words by LORENZ HART
Music by RICHARD RODGERS

MY YIDDISHE MOMME

Words by JACK YELLEN
Music by LEW POLLACK and JACK YELLEN

NEAPOLITAN NIGHTS

Words by HARRY D. KERR
Music by J.S. ZAMECNIK

REFRAIN

Oh, nights of splen-dor,___ Your charms so ten - der___ Make love sur-rend - er___ Till stars are gone; ___ Oh, nights of laugh - ter, ___ Tho' tears come af - ter, ___ Love's re-grets, love for - gets When comes the dawn. ___ Fair' Na - ples

NOBODY KNOWS YOU WHEN YOU'RE DOWN AND OUT

Words and Music by
JIMMIE COX

*Symbols for Guitar, Diagrams for Ukulele.

SAY IT WITH MUSIC

Words and Music by
IRVING BERLIN

SOMEONE TO WATCH OVER ME
(From "OH, KAY!")

Music and Lyrics by
GEORGE and IRA GERSHWIN

REFRAIN

a tempo

There's a some-bod-y I'm long-ing to see. I hope that he Turns out to be

Some-one who'll watch o-ver me. I'm a lit-tle lamb who's

lost in the wood. I know I could Al-ways be good To one who'll

watch o-ver me. Al-though he may not be the

THE SONG IS ENDED
(BUT THE MELODY LINGERS ON)

Words and Music by
IRVING BERLIN

SUNNY
(From "SUNNY")

Lyrics by OSCAR HAMMERSTEIN II and OTTO HARBACH
Music by JEROME KERN

SUNNY SIDE UP

Words and Music by B.G. DeSYLVA,
LEW BROWN and RAY HENDERSON

THOU SWELL
(From "A CONNECTICUT YANKEE")

Words by LORENZ HART
Music by RICHARD RODGERS

WHAT'LL I DO?

Words and Music by
IRVING BERLIN

your way and I must go mine._____ But
my lips were tied with a kiss._____ A

now that our love dreams have end -
kiss with an un - hap - py end -

ed, {
ing. { What-'ll I do _____ when you _____ are far _____ a-

way _____ and I _____ am blue, what-'ll I do._____

WITH A SONG IN MY HEART

(From "SPRING IS HERE")

Words by LORENZ HART
Music by RICHARD RODGERS

YES SIR, THAT'S MY BABY

Lyrics by GUS KAHN
Music by WALTER DONALDSON

YOU ARE LOVE
(From "SHOW BOAT")

Lyrics by OSCAR HAMMERSTEIN II
Music by JEROME KERN

Once a wan-d'ring ne'er-do-well, Just a va-grant rov-ing fel-low, I went my way. Life was just a joke to tell, Like a lone-ly Pun-chi-nel-lo, My role

Poco agitato

Then___ my for - tune turned and I found you;

Here ___ you are with my arms a - round you.

You ___ will nev - er know what you've meant___ to me.

You're ___ the prize that heav - en has sent ___ to me.

Here's ___ a bright and beau-ti-ful world ___ all new Wrapped

Tempo di Valse

up ___ in you. ___

Refrain *(with expression)*

You ___ are love, here in my arms

Where you be-long, And here you will stay. I'll not let you a-

WHO?
(From "SUNNY")

Lyrics by OTTO HARBACH and OSCAR HAMMERSTEIN II
Music by JEROME KERN